A New True Book

PIGEONS AND DOVES

By Ray Nofsinger and Jim Hargrove

CHILDRENS PRESS®
CHICAGO

Pigeons can be seen
all year long.

PHOTO CREDITS

© Virginia R. Grimes—4 (top right & bottom)

H. Armstrong Roberts—© Camerique, 12

© Jim Hargrove—11, 16 (top), 19, 21, 26, 33
(2 photos), 34 (2 photos), 36, 39, 40 (2 photos), 41,
42, 44

Historical Pictures—22 (2 photos)

Photo Researchers, Inc.—© Tom McHugh, 14
(2 photos)

Photri—23; © Mark G. Myers, Cover Inset;
© Leonard Lee Rue, 9

Root Resources—© Earl L. Kubis, 13 (right)

Tom Stack & Associates—© Shattil/Rozinski, 4
(top left); © Bill Everitt, 15 (bottom left)

SuperStock International, Inc.—© Medford Taylor,
Cover, 8 (right); © Eric Carle, 2

TSW-CLICK/Chicago—© Bob Thomason, 7

Valan—© Karen D. Rooney, 8 (left); © J. R. Page, 15
(right); © Pam Hickman, 16 (bottom); © John
Fowler, 25, 28 (2 photos), 30; © Richard T. Nowitz,
45 (right)

Visuals Unlimited—© John D. Cunningham, 6;
© Arthur R. Hill, 13 (left), 15 (top left); © Stephen W.
Kress, 24; © Bruce Iverson, 45 (left)

Cover—Pigeon at water fountain

Cover Inset—Pigeon on nest

Library of Congress Cataloging-in-Publication Data

Nofsinger, Ray.
  Pigeons and doves / by Ray Nofsinger and Jim
Hargrove.
      p.   cm. — (A New true book)
  Includes index.
  Summary: An introduction to pigeons, discussing
physical characteristics, the talents of homing pigeons,
and pet care.
  ISBN 0-516-02196-6
    1. Pigeons—Juvenile literature.   2.   Homing
pigeons—Juvenile literature.   [1.   Pigeons.
2. Homing pigeons.]   I. Hargrove, Jim.
II. Title. III. Series.
SF465.35.N64   1992
636.5'96—dc20   92-12948
                                              CIP
                                              AC

TABLE OF CONTENTS

Pigeons live in many countries. Top left: Pigeon houses in Egypt. Top right: A man feeds pigeons in London, England. Bottom: White doves live at a mission in California.

THE PIGEON FAMILY

Pigeons live in most countries of the world. Some pigeons live in cities. Others live in the country.

There are hundreds of different kinds of birds in the pigeon family. Medium and large birds in this family are called pigeons. Smaller birds in the same family are sometimes called doves.

Rock dove

It is easy to tell whether a bird is a pigeon. Pigeons have soft, white bumps of skin on their beaks. Most other birds do not. The bumps are sometimes called ceres.

Mourning dove
and baby chick
in the nest

WILD PIGEONS AND PET PIGEONS

Pigeons can live almost anywhere. In the country, wild pigeons often build nests in barns, under bridges, and even in trees or on the ground. They eat fruits and seeds. Sometimes they eat insects.

7

City pigeons gather around
a statue (left). A pigeon drinks
from a park fountain (above).

Many wild pigeons also
live in cities. They can be
found perched on buildings,
water towers, statues–just
about anywhere.

The mourning dove is a
small wild pigeon. It is

The mourning dove is named for its low, sad call.

found throughout North America.

People have kept pigeons as pets for thousands of years. Some pigeons are kept because of their fancy feathers and colors. Others—such as tumbler and roller pigeons–are trained to do backflips and other stunts.

But there is a more important reason for keeping pigeons. It has to do with a special talent some pigeons have.

Even when taken far away, some pigeons can fly straight back home. They hardly ever seem to get lost. This kind of bird is called a homing pigeon.

Owners don't care how their homing pigeons look. They want birds that are speedy fliers and can find their way home.

PLAIN AND FANCY FEATHERS

Homing pigeons, sometimes called homers, can be almost any color. Most are brown, white, or grey. Homing pigeons look much like wild pigeons.

White fantail pigeon

Some pigeons have
fancy feathers. The fantail
pigeon is named for the
fan-shaped feathers that
make up its tail.

The crowned pigeon is
named for its beautiful

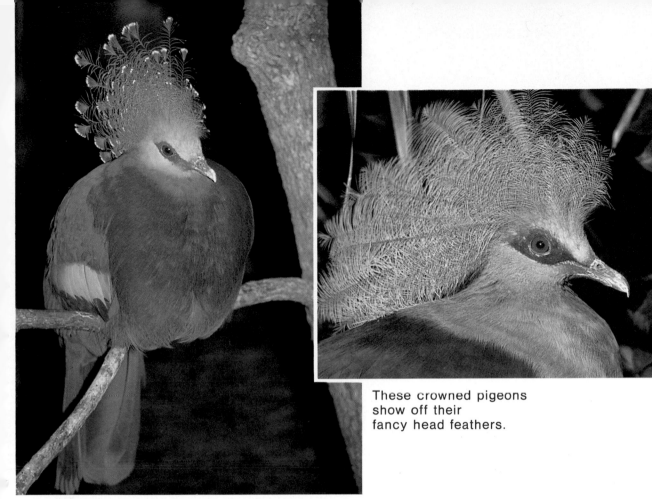

These crowned pigeons
show off their
fancy head feathers.

head feathers. It is the
largest bird in the pigeon
family.

The Jacobin pigeon has
feathers that form a hood

The Jacobin pigeon
(above) and the
double-crested
trumpeter (right) are
beautiful birds.

on the back of its head.
The double-crested
trumpeter seems to have
wings on its feet. This
strange look is caused by
feathers that grow out of
its legs.

14

Most common pigeons are descended from rock doves (below). Can you tell how the pink-necked fruit dove (left) and the bleeding-heart pigeon (below left) got their names?

The rock dove has black stripes on its wings and tail, and colorful green and purple neck feathers.

15

Pigeon eggs (above). The egg on top is about to hatch.
The new babies (below) are often called squeakers because
of the sounds they make.

SQUEAKERS

People often call baby pigeons squeakers. The name comes from the little squeaking noises the babies make.

Unless they are separated, pigeons mate for life. The female pigeon is called a hen. She usually lays two eggs at a time. The babies hatch about eighteen days after the eggs are laid. They are born without feathers, and their eyes are closed.

Squeakers only live with their parents for four or five weeks. Then, they are pushed out of the nest. At the same time, the parent birds prepare to have more eggs.

At four or five weeks old, squeakers are not good fliers. But they soon

Young pigeons can fly about four
or five weeks after they hatch.

learn how to fly well and
take care of themselves.
Several months later the
squeakers will be old
enough to have babies of
their own.   **19**

THE TALENTED HOMING PIGEON

For thousands of years, people have known that homing pigeons have a rare skill. They are born with the ability to find their way home from places they have never been before. Some pigeons have flown thousands of miles to return to their homes.

Scientists do not know

A group of homing pigeons in flight

how homing pigeons find
their way home. Some
think the birds can feel
the magnetic field that
surrounds the Earth.
Others think that pigeons
get their direction from the
location of the sun.
Pigeons rarely fly at night.

Homing pigeons are sometimes called carrier pigeons.
Left: A bird carries a message in ancient Rome.
Right: A carrier pigeon is sent on its way in the Middle Ages.

HOMERS IN HISTORY

The ancient Egyptians kept pigeons five thousand years ago. In 776 B.C. pigeons brought news of the Olympic Games held in Greece.

From A.D. 1150 to 1258, homers delivered mail regularly in the city of

22

In World War I, the U.S. Army used pigeons to send messages on the battlefield. These soldiers carry pigeon cages on their backs.

Baghdad. In the twentieth century, homing pigeons were used to carry messages in both world wars. A pigeon trained by the U.S. Army Signal Corps flew home from a distance of 2,300 miles (3701 kilometers).

23

Wild pigeons like to sit on windowsills or ledges on tall buildings.

WHERE DO PIGEONS LIVE?

Wild pigeons can live almost anywhere where they are protected from bad weather and from other animals.

Pet pigeons live in a special house called a loft.

Pet pigeons have a special kind of home called a loft. Some people build lofts in their backyards. A loft the size of a toolshed can hold up to one hundred birds.

Inside the loft, the birds perch in special boxes.

City people can make a loft not much larger than a bread box. This little loft will hold one or two pigeons. Even in cold weather, lofts are not heated. But they must be kept dry and airy.

CARING FOR PET PIGEONS

People who raise pigeons must work hard. To keep their birds healthy, the pigeon loft and its food and water containers must be kept clean.

The birds are usually fed and given water twice a day. Pigeons often eat a mixture of dry corn, peas, safflower and flax seeds, among other things.

Fancy birds are allowed to eat as much as they

Pigeons feed mainly on dried seeds and grains.

want. Homers that are being trained to race are given smaller amounts of food.

Pigeons are also given vitamins and medicine. Once a year, every pet pigeon needs shots as protection against certain diseases.

28

TRAINING CHAMPION FLIERS

For the first few months, baby birds never leave the loft. After that, they are allowed outside.

Most owners release their birds at least once a day, if the weather is nice. Usually, the birds fly in big circles high above the loft.

A racing pigeon being placed in the basket

When the young birds are strong enough to stay up for one to two hours, they are ready for training.

Homers are carefully picked up and placed in a basket. The basket is then taken by car a short

distance from the loft.
Then the basket is opened
so that the birds can fly
home.

Distances are slowly
increased. Within a month
or so, the birds may fly
50 miles (80 kilometers) or
more to get home. At this
point, homers are ready to
enter races. Owners often
keep records that show
how each bird flies during
training.

GETTING READY TO RACE

The day before a race, birds are fed and watered. The owner decides which birds will race the next day.

The birds about to race are placed in baskets and taken to a clubhouse. A tiny rubber band, called a counter mark, is placed on a leg of each racing pigeon. Each counter mark has a different number.

As each bird is marked,

Each pigeon in the race wears
a counter mark (left) on one leg.
Pigeons (above) wait for the truck.

it is put into a crate with
other pigeons. At the club,
there may be dozens of
crates filled with racers.

When it's time, the birds
are placed on a truck with
birds from other clubs.
Several thousand homers

Homing pigeons ride to the race point in a special truck. Inset: A pigeon-racing clock

may be carried in a single truck. When the loading is completed at the last club, the truck drives to the race point. Sometimes, the truck must drive all night. The race point is usually between 80 and 500 miles (129 and 805 kilometers) away.

Back at the clubhouses, people make final checks of their clocks. In pigeon racing, clocks are sealed boxes with timepieces built into them. All clocks must be set to exactly the same time. They will be used to prove which bird won the race.

When the clocks are set, pigeon owners go home. The great race is about to begin.

The race begins! Two thousand pigeons are being
released from this truck to start the flight home.

THE GREAT RACE

Very early in the morning, the truck carrying thousands of pigeons reaches the race point. The driver opens the truck doors. The pigeons can see outside, but they are not yet free to fly.

Soon after dawn, all the pigeons are released at the same time. They may need a few minutes to decide which way to go. If in doubt, they will fly in big circles until they know which direction leads home.

Homing pigeons are very strong fliers. Some can fly in a long 500-mile (805-kilometer) race without stopping. Homers usually fly at speeds up to 50 miles (80 kilometers) per hour. A few can fly faster.

Birds do not have to follow roads, or stop for traffic lights. Even a race

Homing pigeon
in flight

car cannot beat a homing
pigeon flying back to its loft.

At home, owners watch
the sky for their homers.
The excitement builds as
time passes.

Soon, the first bird
arrives at the loft. Sometimes
several birds arrive at
about the same time.

Pigeons landing near the trap. They are not officially "home" until they go inside the loft.

Most well-trained birds enter their lofts quickly. They go in through a one-way door called a trap. Sometimes, birds do not go inside right away. This makes owners nervous. The race is not over until a bird enters its loft and is clocked.

When the bird enters the loft, the counter mark is removed from its leg and dropped into the clock.

Inside the loft, the owner removes the rubber counter mark from the bird's leg. The counter mark is dropped into an opening in the clock. The clock makes a printed note of the time each counter mark is put inside.

Adjusting a clock at the pigeon club

AND THE WINNER IS

When the last time is
recorded, the owners take
their clocks to the club.
After everyone arrives, the
clocks are opened. The

times on the printed notes inside the clocks are entered into a small computer.

The computer helps adjust times for slight differences in clocks. Each loft is at a slightly different distance from the race point. The computer also helps figure the flight speed of each bird. The speed is based on flight distance and flight time.

Ray Nofsinger and his pigeon-racing trophies

When all the figuring is done, the winner is announced. Winning birds earn trophies and sometimes cash prizes for their owners.

Pigeons have unusual talents. Living in the wild, they can adapt to both

city and country life. As pets, they can do many things. But the most interesting talent is the ability of homing pigeons to find their way back home!

WORDS YOU SHOULD KNOW

adjust (uh • JUST) — to make small changes in something

ancient Egyptians (AIN • shint ee • JIP • shunz) — the people who lived in Egypt thousands of years ago

cere (SEER) — a bump of skin at the base of a bird's beak

computer (kum • PYOO • ter) — a machine that does calculations and keeps track of records

crate (KRAIT) — a box made from slats of wood with spaces between them

dove (DUV) — a small bird in the pigeon family

flax (FLAX) — a flowering plant whose seeds have a rich oil

Jacobin (JAK • uh • bin) — a type of fancy pigeon

magnetic field (mag • NEH • tik FEELD) — the space around a magnet in which the force of the magnet is felt

safflower (SAFF • flower) — a plant like a thistle with orange flowers and oil-rich seeds

skill (SKILL) — a special ability gained by practice or study

talent (TAL • int) — a natural ability

timepieces (TYME • peeces) — machines that tell time, such as clocks or watches

trophies (TRO • feez) — statues, cups, etc., given to show that someone has won a race or contest

vitamins (VY • tuh • minz) — substances that the body needs for normal growth and health

INDEX

About the Authors

Ray Nofsinger is a 20-year-old pigeon racer who lives in northern Illinois. He has been raising and racing pigeons since 1984 and has won numerous junior races and, so far, two senior races. He is a member of the American Racing Pigeon Union, Inc.

Jim Hargrove is a free-lance writer who has written more than thirty books for Childrens Press and has contributed to the works of many other publishers. To take photographs for this book, Hargrove chased pigeons across all of northern Illinois.

The American Racing Pigeon Union, Inc.

The American Racing Pigeon Union, P.O. Box 2713, South Hamilton, MA 01982, is a nationwide organization of local racing clubs. It establishes and publishes guidelines for the sport of pigeon racing.